MONSTER ⚙ MACHINES

SPACECRAFT

DAVID JEFFERIS

RAINTREE
STECK-VAUGHN
PUBLISHERS

A Harcourt Company

Austin   New York
www.steck-vaughn.com

Library of Congress Cataloging-in-Publication Data
Jefferis, David.
  Spacecraft / David Jefferis.
  p. cm.—(Monster machines)
  Includes index.
  ISBN 0-7398-2881-9
  1. Space vehicles—Juvenile literature. [1. Space vehicles.]
  I. Title. II. Series.

TL793 .J44 2001
629.47—dc21
                        00-056132

Printed in Singapore
Bound in the United States
1 2 3 4 5 6 7 8 9 0   02 01 00

Acknowledgments
We wish to thank the following individuals and organizations for their help and assistance and for supplying material in their collections: Alpha Archive, Arianespace, Beagle 2 image ©Beagle 2 http://beagle2.open.ac.uk, JPL Jet Propulsion Laboratory, ESA European Space Agency, Kistler Aerospace Corp., Lockheed Martin Corp., Lockheed Martin Skunk Works, NASA Space Agency, National Space Science Data Center, Orbital Sciences Corp., Boris Rabin, RKA Russian Space Agency, Space Island Group

Illustrations and diagrams by Gavin Page

▲ A future *X-33* space plane glides back to base.

CONTENTS

⚙ TECH TALK
Look for the cog and blue box for explanations of technical terms.

👁 EYE VIEW
Look for the eye and yellow box for eyewitness accounts.

ROCKET INTO SPACE

Spacecraft leave the Earth onboard a rocket launcher. Powerful motors are needed for liftoff and to fly high into space.

▲ The first astronaut, Yuri Gagarin, flew onboard a *Vostok* rocket in 1961.

Rocket motors use a fuel, such as liquid hydrogen. Inside the motor, the hydrogen fuel is mixed with liquid oxygen, the fuel which makes it burn. A powerful flame roars out of the motor, and this pushes the rocket forward.

Rockets are built in several parts, or stages. Each booster stage has its own engines and falls away when its fuel is used. Most rockets have three stages.

Using its lower stages to gain speed, a rocket has to reach more than 17,400 miles per hour (28,000 kph) to fly into space. If it goes slower, it will fall back to Earth.

The satellite is carried in the top section.

booster stages

rocket engines

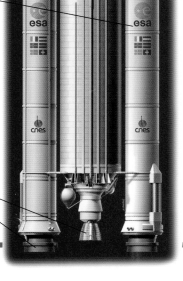

◀ The *Ariane 5* rocket has two boosters, on either side of the main body. These fall away when their fuel is used up. The center engine keeps going until the Ariane goes into space. The satellite load is carried in the top part.

👁 THE ROAR OF LIFTOFF

"Seeing a big rocket leave the ground is awe-inspiring. We watched an *Ariane* from 3 miles (5 km) away. First, you see billowing smoke, then flames from the base of the rocket. It starts to lift off, and only then do you hear the sound. It's an earth-shaking wall of noise, an avalanche. Your whole body is pounded by roaring waves of sound. I've never felt so small!" *Photographer*

◀ The *Ariane 5* rocket can lift a big load into space. The load could be one big spacecraft or several small ones. *Ariane* rockets are launched from Kourou, a space base in the jungles of South America.

SATELLITES IN ORBIT

▲ The first artificial satellite was called *Sputnik 1*. It was launched in 1957.

A satellite is any space object that circles around, or orbits, another larger one. Today hundreds of satellites orbit the Earth.

Before rockets were invented, Earth had just one satellite, the Moon. It orbits 240,000 miles (386,000 km) away from our planet.

Today the Moon is not alone. Hundreds of artificial satellites orbit much closer to the Earth. These satellites carry out many jobs. For example, some send back information about pollution or about the weather. Other satellites beam radio and TV signals around the world.

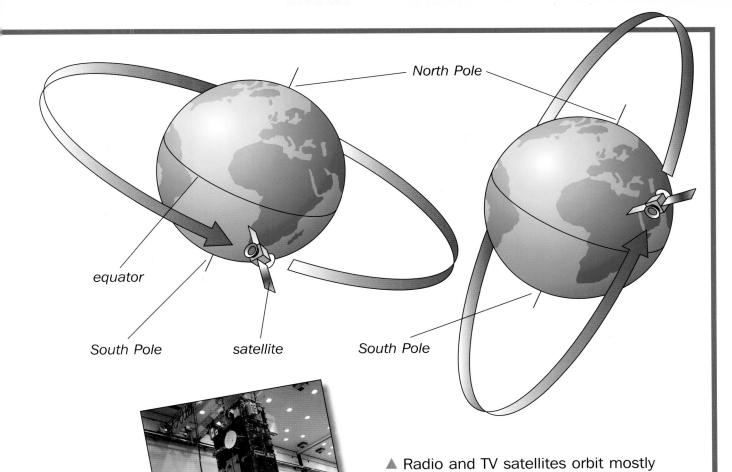

North Pole

equator

South Pole   satellite   South Pole

Solar cells supply power by changing the energy in sunlight to electricity.

▲ Radio and TV satellites orbit mostly above the equator. Weather satellites often orbit over the poles.

◄ Technicians prepare satellites carefully. When it is ready, this weather satellite will be placed onboard a rocket launcher.

◄ This satellite beams radio signals between cellular phones in Europe and North Africa.

⚙ BIGGER AND BIGGER

Sputnik 1 measured just 24 inches (60 cm) across and weighed about 185 pounds (84 kg). The biggest TV satellite today is over 70 feet (52 m) across. The spread of its solar-cell "wings" is about the same as the wingspan of a medium-sized jet airliner.

LAUNCHING THE SHUTTLE

The space shuttle is the only rocket that can carry up to seven astronauts into space.

▲ The orbiter is flown on a 747 jetliner to the launch site at Cape Canaveral.

The space shuttle has several main parts. The orbiter looks like a chunky aircraft and carries astronauts and cargo, such as a satellite. For takeoff, the orbiter's three main engines suck fuel from a huge external tank (ET). Two solid-rocket boosters (SRBs) are attached to the external tank. Once started, they burn fiercely until empty.

◀ Before launch, the loaded orbiter is joined to the big external tank and smaller solid boosters. Here they are shown on the mobile launch pad, which takes the shuttle to the takeoff area.

▶ Shuttle mission 96 takes off with a massive roar.

At takeoff, the orbiter's main engines and the two SRBs burn together. After two minutes, the SRBs are used up. They fall into the ocean, to be collected later by ships. The orbiter flies on, using fuel from the ET. When this is empty, it falls into the ocean, too.

The external tank holds fuel for the orbiter's main engines.

⚙ LIFTING A MONSTER WEIGHT
Fueled and loaded for a space mission, the complete space shuttle weighs over 2,000 tons. A lot of power is needed to lift this weight off the ground. Each SRB gives 1,300 tons of thrust for just over two minutes. The orbiter's three main engines burn until the external tank is empty. Then two smaller engines give a final shove into orbit.

Solid rocket boosters burn for 123 seconds.

SURVIVAL IN SPACE

Earth is the only place where humans can live without protection. Out in space astronauts need special equipment to survive.

▲ In 1970 U.S. astronauts narrowly escaped disaster when oxygen tanks in their *Apollo 13* spacecraft exploded.

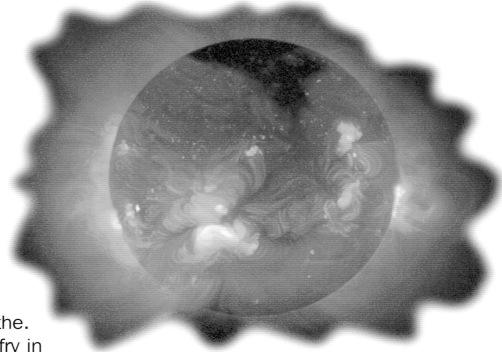

In space there is no air to breathe. You would fry in the Sun's heat, or freeze in ice-cold shadows. A spacecraft such as the shuttle orbiter is designed to carry astronauts in comfort. It holds air, food, and water for a space mission of a week or more.

When astronauts leave the orbiter, they have to wear a spacesuit. Its backpack holds enough supplies for the astronaut to work in space for several hours.

▲ The Sun gives us heat and light. Both are needed for life. But the Sun also sends out invisible rays that can kill an unprotected astronaut.

✿ HOT AND COLD IN SPACE

Parts of a spacecraft in the full glare of the Sun can reach a scorching 250°F (122°C). In the shadows, temperatures may drop to −290°F (−180°C). Spacecraft on long missions often go into "barbecue mode." This is a slow roll that evens out these hot and cold extremes.

▲ Shuttle astronaut Bruce McCandless floats in space, 185 miles (300 km) above the Earth. His backpack has gas thrusters. He can use these to move about in any direction.

SPACE WORKERS

Shuttle astronauts are kept busy when they fly into space. Their jobs range from launching satellites to observing our planet.

▲ Shuttle astronauts wear lightweight flight suits, except during takeoff and landing.

The shuttle orbiter has a big cargo bay for carrying satellites. Cargo bay doors open, so the satellites can be launched into space.

Satellites can also be brought in for repair. If astronauts need to work on a satellite, they put on spacesuits and work just outside the orbiter.

Astronauts train for these repairs before their mission leaves the ground. Then they know exactly what to do when they are floating in space.

▲ Even hair floats during flight in orbit. Some people wear hair nets to keep things neat and tidy.

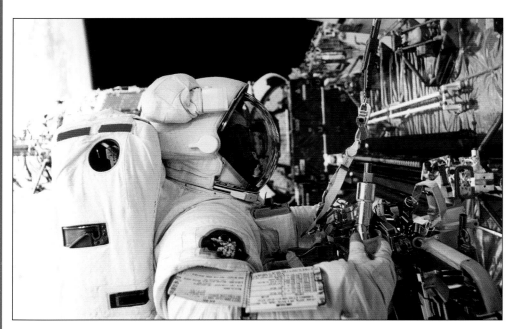

◄ Here an astronaut services a satellite in the orbiter's cargo bay. A work checklist is clipped to the right arm.

▲ A small satellite is launched from a shuttle orbiter's open cargo bay.

⚙ FLOATING IN FREE FALL

There is no feeling of weight in orbit. Inside a spacecraft, objects float about freely unless they are tied down. This is called zero gravity, or being in free fall. Most astronauts enjoy free fall, although many feel sick until they get used to the feeling. They may have to take anti-sickness medicine for the first few days.

SPACE STATION

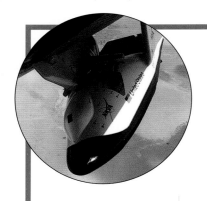

▲ The X-38 is a space lifeboat for ISS crews.

The International Space Station (ISS) will be the biggest space station ever built for a space crew once it is finished.

The ISS is made up of parts that come from many places, including the United States, Russia, Japan, and Europe.

▲ The first parts of the ISS were placed in orbit during 1999.

The ISS goes around our world once every 80 minutes, so astronauts can carry out many observations. Astronauts also practice spacewalks and carry out experiments on the effects of zero gravity on living things. Plants may grow straggly. Human bones may become weak and brittle.

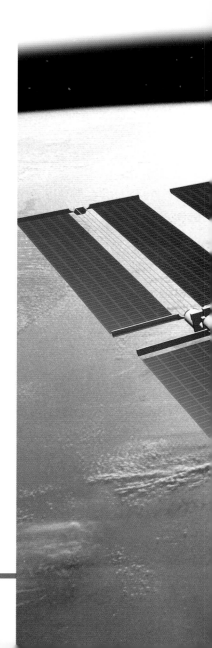

► The International Space Station will be huge when it is finished. The "wings" are solar cells. These make electricity from the energy contained in sunlight.

◉ WHY IS A SPACE STATION NOISY?

"The noise onboard the Russian *Mir (Peace)* space station was caused mainly by the dozens of electric fans. They were needed to circulate air or cool equipment. It was a bit like being in a noisy airplane, or the engine room of a boat. During my stay, I forgot what silence was like!" *French astronaut*

▲ Many astronauts have visited Russia's *Mir* space station.

space lifeboat docked at the ISS

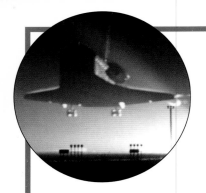

▲ Night landing for a shuttle orbiter.

FIERY REENTRY

Spacecraft return from orbit through the atmosphere. When they hit the air at very high speed, they glow with heat.

Returning spacecraft hit the upper layer of Earth's atmosphere at about 17,400 mph (28,000 kph). Rubbing against air particles at this speed creates great heat. Shuttle orbiters are protected by heatproof materials. The shuttle crew can see the scorching-hot air hurtling past the cabin windows.

Parts of the orbiter reach 3,000°F (1,650°C).

▲ The hottest parts of the orbiter are the nose area and front edges of the wings.

FROM TAKEOFF TO LANDING

1. The Kistler cargo rocket is designed to be reused after a flight in orbit. Back at base, the Kistler can be refueled for another flight.

2. The stages separate after the launch.

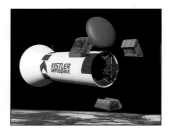

3. The satellite is placed into orbit.

When the orbiter has slowed to below 8,080 mph (13,000 kph), it starts to fly as a glider. Touchdown is at a steady 215 mph (346 kph). On the runway a parachute is released to slow the orbiter. Wheel brakes bring the spacecraft to a stop.

◉ WATCHING A SHUTTLE LAND

"The scary thing about seeing an orbiter coming in to land is just how late the wheels are lowered! The space plane gets nearer and nearer, and just when you're convinced it's going to belly flop on the runway, the wheels go down. But that's only 14 seconds before touchdown! On the runway, a parachute pops out from the tail." *Photographer*

4. Rockets are fired to slow down the spacecraft.

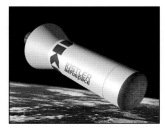

5. The front end glows with heat at reentry.

6. Parachutes open to slow the fall.

7. Air cushions allow a soft landing.

SPACE TELESCOPE

The Hubble Space Telescope (HST) views the heavens as it orbits Earth. It is above the atmosphere, so the pictures it takes are not ruined by dust in the air.

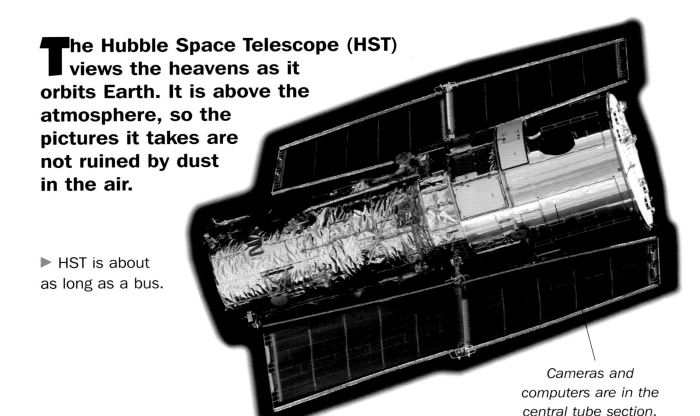

▶ HST is about as long as a bus.

Cameras and computers are in the central tube section.

The Hubble Space Telescope can peer far into space. Its powerful cameras show us close-ups of other planets, or of new stars being formed from gas and dust. The pictures here are just three of the thousands HST has taken since it was launched in 1990.

▶ An HST picture of huge gas clouds, far away in space.

▷ Shuttle astronauts have serviced the HST several times. Here it sits in an orbiter's cargo bay.

▽ The planet Saturn looks like a giant Easter egg in this HST photo. Special filters make it look as if it is brightly colored. To our eyes, Saturn appears a pale creamy color.

▽ The desert planet Mars

MARS EXPLORERS

▲ Mars (right) is a smaller world than the Earth.

Spacecraft first searched for life on Mars in the 1970s. Other machines have been sent since.

In 1976 two *Viking* craft landed on Mars to look for signs of life. They did not find any Martians.

However, Mars does have dried-up river valleys. Scientists think that if there was water millions of years ago, there may also have been some sort of Martian life.

Rover machines from Earth may one day find the age-old remains of Martian creatures.

◉ DRIVING A MARS ROVER

"*Sojourner* was the U.S. rover that explored Mars in 1997. We called the rover Rocky, and it lasted nearly three months instead of a week as planned. The driver was Brian Cooper, and he had some problems. Rocky went in circles, tried to climb a boulder, and nearly got stuck in a crack. Even so, Cooper kept the rover out of trouble." *Technician*

Rocky explored Mars in 1997.

▼ Fido 3 is a design for a future Mars rover.

◀ The *Beagle 2* space probe is designed to dig into the Martian soil. Scientists hope it may find signs of life under the surface.

Fido 3 is about the size of a microwave oven.

INTO DEEP SPACE

The giant planets Jupiter and Saturn are huge balls of gas, with no solid surface. Spacecraft have visited both of them.

▲ Jupiter (left) and Saturn are far bigger than Earth (arrowed). They are far from the Sun and ice cold.

The *Galileo* spacecraft launched a probe into the clouds of Jupiter in 1995. The probe lasted for a while but was soon crushed by the gases in Jupiter's atmosphere.

Galileo still cruises near Jupiter, taking pictures of the planet and its 16 moons.

Jupiter space probe is inside this protective cover.

▲ Technicians check *Cassini* before it leaves for Saturn.

◄ *Cassini* launches the *Huygens* lander.

Cassini is a spacecraft sent to the ringed planet Saturn. It also has a probe, named *Huygens*. This will land on Titan, one of Saturn's moons. *Huygens* will explore under Titan's smoggy clouds.

⚙ **MESSAGES FROM SPACE**

Radio signals travel at 186,420 miles (300,000 km) per second. But distances in space are vast, so a message from a space probe near Jupiter may take more than 10 hours to arrive. The faint signals are picked up on Earth by giant telescopes like these.

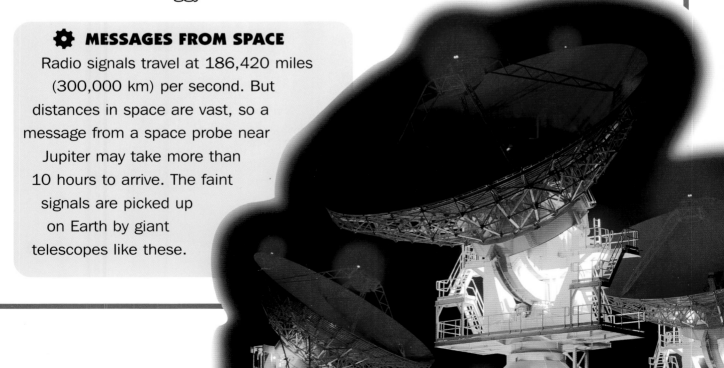

FANTASTIC FUTURE

There are plans for future spacecraft that will make spaceflight cheaper and safer.

Future spacecraft may make space trips almost as common as flying by jetliner today. Some companies have come up with detailed plans for hotels in space, and even a huge leisure center on the Moon.

The *VentureStar* may replace the space shuttle. It should be able to fly into space without throwing away empty fuel tanks, helping to make missions cheaper.

▲ A test model for a future shuttle leaves the ground.

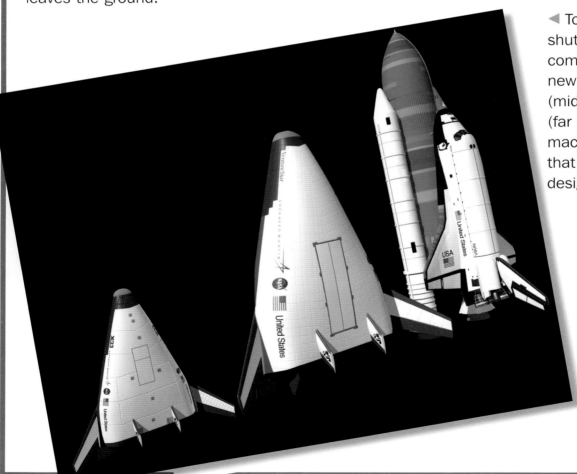

◀ Today's space shuttle (right), compared with the new *VentureStar* (middle). The *X-33* (far left) is a test machine to prove that *VentureStar's* design will work.

⚙ THE FLYING TRAFFIC CONE

The *Roton* is a strange-looking spacecraft that looks similar to a traffic cone. The two-person *Roton*, seen here in a trial run, has a rocket engine in the base for takeoff. If all goes to plan, it will fly into space using rocket power. For landing, the *Roton* has a set of fold-out helicopter rotors. With these spinning around, the pilot should be able to steer the *Roton* to a gentle landing.

crew cabin

► A future crewed spacecraft arrives at Mars after the long trip from Earth.

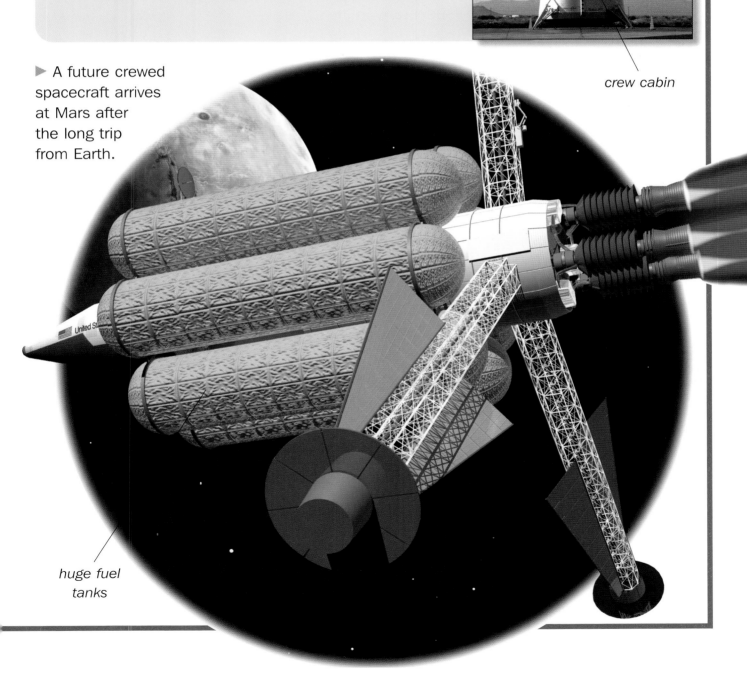

huge fuel tanks

SPACECRAFT FACTS

Here are some facts and figures from the world of spaceflight.

▲ This design shows a space hotel made from empty space shuttle fuel tanks.

Dogs in space
A dog called Laika became the first living thing in orbit when the Russians flew her onboard a *Vostok* rocket in November 1957. Sadly, no plans were made to bring her back to Earth.

Jet launcher
A converted jet airliner is used to launch the *X-34* rocket-plane. The *X-34* is hung under the jet before flight. After takeoff, the plane climbs to 39,370 feet (12,000 m), when the commander presses a button to drop the uncrewed *X-34*. After a few moments, its rocket motor fires, and the *X-34* soars upward. The TriStar is really a booster that flies back to base, rather than being wasted.

Danger—paint in space!
Bits of old space rocket can be a danger. In 1993 a fleck of paint from another rocket hit a space shuttle orbiter. The collision speed was 37 miles (60 km) per second. A super-tough window pane was cracked.

Star tours
Space tourism could be big business in the future. Plans include short flights to "the edge of space" for $90,000. There is also an idea for a space hotel made from used space shuttle fuel tanks.

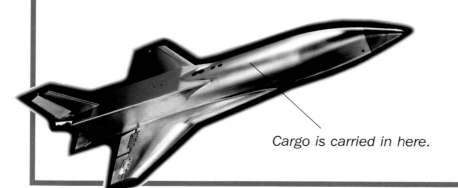

Cargo is carried in here.

◀ The *X-34* looks similar to the shuttle orbiter, but it is smaller and sleeker. It is computer-controlled and carries no astronauts.

Lighting-up time

Astronauts working outside the space shuttle need spacesuits with headlights. Every other 45 minutes is spent in darkness because the spacecraft passes through the Earth's shadow. After that it's 45 minutes of sunshine again.

Personal assistant

Astronauts onboard the International Space Station (ISS) may be helped by a basketball-shaped PSA, or personal satellite assistant. The PSA will check on air quality in the ISS, as well as have video cameras and microphones.

Toilets in space

Early astronauts had to make do with diapers in their tiny spacecraft. During Apollo trips to the Moon in the 1960s, astronauts put human waste into sealed bags. Today's shuttle crews use a space toilet, which sucks waste away to be stored. It can be used four times an hour.

▲ In the future, spacecraft may take off along a long, high-speed track.

Oil-rig rocket

Perhaps the oddest place to launch a spacecraft is from the middle of the ocean. But the Sea Launch system uses a converted oil rig as a floating launchpad. The people who run Sea Launch say the oil rig is cheaper to use than a big base on land.

Space submarine

Planners are designing a mini-submarine to explore under the ice of Jupiter's moon Europa. They think there may be a vast ocean of water under the frozen surface. Some scientists believe that if there is water, there may be life.

▲ Sea Launch rockets take off from a converted oil rig.

SPACECRAFT WORDS

Here are some technical terms used in this book.

atmosphere
(AT-muh-sfear)
The layer of air that surrounds our planet. It is made mostly of the gases nitrogen and oxygen. In space there is no air, so astronauts must carry supplies to breathe.

backpack
A spacesuit's life support system. It carries an air supply, heating and cooling systems, plus a radio, for communication. Some suits have a gas thruster system, too, for moving freely in space.

booster stage
A motor system that helps a rocket take off and speed up to space. Most rockets use three boosters, each stage falling away when its fuel is used up.

cargo bay
An area in the center of a space shuttle where satellites are carried.

free fall
The floating of objects caused by zero gravity in orbit.

Hubble Space Telescope
A computerized telescope that orbits Earth. It is named after the American astronomer Edwin Hubble.

liquid hydrogen
(LI-qwid HIGH-druh-jen)
Hydrogen gas that is cooled until it becomes liquid. It can be stored in a rocket fuel tank and burned.

▶ The nine planets are shown here, to scale for size with the much bigger Sun. Distances are not shown to scale. At this size, Earth would be several miles from the Sun.

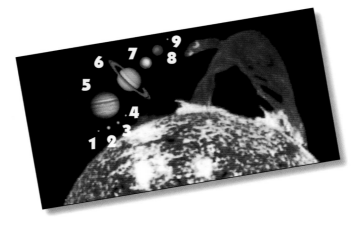

Planets shown are: 1 Mercury, 2 Venus, 3 Earth, 4 Mars, 5 Jupiter, 6 Saturn, 7 Uranus, 8 Neptune, 9 Pluto

orbit

The path taken by one space object around another, bigger one. Space shuttles orbit the Earth at about 150 miles (240 km). The Moon orbits the Earth 240,000 miles (385,000 km) away.

reentry

(ree-en-tree) Coming back into the Earth's atmosphere at the end of a space mission. Spacecraft reenter at about 17,400 mph (28,000 kph). They need protection so that they do not burn in the upper air. The shuttle orbiter has tiles that can resist the heat.

rover

The general name for any space probe that can move around on another planet. The first rover on Mars was Rocky.

satellite

(SAT-uhl-light) Any space object that orbits another. It may be a human-made satellite, or a natural one.

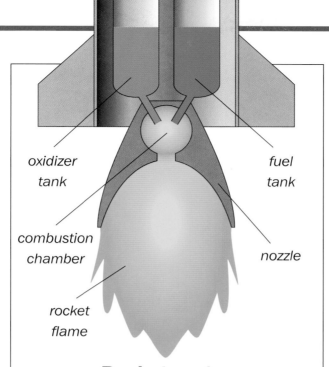

oxidizer tank

fuel tank

combustion chamber

nozzle

rocket flame

Rocket motor

A rocket motor works by mixing fuel (such as liquid hydrogen) with an oxidizer (such as liquid oxygen). When mixed, the two burn in a combustion chamber. Flames roar out of the motor's nozzle, and the thrust from this pushes the rocket forward.

solar cell

A flat panel that uses the energy in the Sun's rays to make electricity. Solar cells are used by many spacecraft for power. They are often mounted on "arms" that unfold like insect wings.

solar system

The group of nine planets and their moons that orbit around the Sun. The solar system also includes many smaller objects, such as comets. These are frozen "snowballs" made of a crumbling mixture of dust, ice, and gas.

space plane

A spacecraft with wings that returns from space to land on a runway, like an aircraft. Future space planes may take off from a runway, and fly into space without needing throwaway boosters.

space probe

Any spacecraft built to fly into deep space on missions to explore distant space objects.

SPACE PROJECTS

These projects show you some of the science behind the world of space and spacecraft.

LOSE SOME WEIGHT!

The Moon is a small world. Objects there weigh six times less than they do on Earth. How heavy would you be if you were an astronaut walking on the Moon? Just weigh yourself, then divide the result by six!

Could you set a Moon high-jump record?

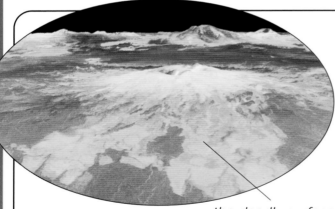

the deadly surface of Venus

THE PRESSURE CRUSHER

The planet Venus has an atmosphere 90 times thicker than that of Earth. Space probes have survived only a short time before being crushed. This project shows pressure in action.

1. A big plastic water bottle is just right for this experiment. Unscrew the top, then pour in some hot water. To be safe, ask an adult to do this.

2. A cupful of hot water should be enough. Swirl the water to heat the inside of the bottle. Now pour the water out, and very quickly reseal the top.

ACTION AND REACTION

Rockets work by the forces of action and reaction. The action is a roaring flame from the engine. The reaction is that the rocket goes quickly in the opposite direction. At takeoff, this is straight up. In space it may be at any angle.

1. Blow up a balloon, then let it go. The action is your breath whizzing out of the neck. The reaction is the balloon flying off.

2. Blow up the balloon to various sizes. Its speed after release depends on the strength of the air jet. Rockets work in a similar way.

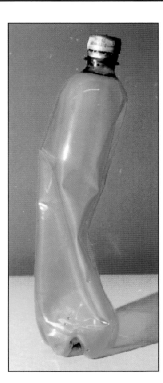

4. The cooling air inside the bottle shrinks back to normal, so there is now less air inside. The air outside is at a higher pressure, and starts to press in on the bottle's sides. You may hear a loud "crack" as the sides of the bottle start to give way.

3. When it heats up, air inside the bottle expands. Some escapes from the top before the cap is screwed back on. As the bottle cools, the air inside cools, too.

5. For dramatic results, use hotter water, and put the bottle in a refrigerator. Like a space probe on Venus, the bottle will be crushed flat.

INDEX